I0101672

The Affair Playbook
What Happens in An Affair?

Angelina & Brad's Divorce
Provides Some Insights

Elizabeth Landers

Copyright © 2017 by Elizabeth Landers

All rights reserved. This book or any portion thereof may not be reproduced or used in any manner whatsoever without the express written permission of the publisher except for the use of brief quotations in a book review or scholarly journal.

First Printing: 2017

ISBN: 978-0-692-91066-5

Larkspur Press
18530 Mack Ave. No. 428
Grosse Pointe Farms, MI 48326

www.elizsays.com

Book Design & Illustration:
Kyle Lewis & Mitch Massu
The UPS Store Grosse Pointe Farms, MI

Introduction

Angelina and Brad are getting divorced. Surprising? It seems that way but it isn't really. Shocking? It is but only because we're not well versed in The Affair Playbook.

We're not well versed because what happens as an affair begins and often comes to its sad conclusion is, below the surface, not a pretty or romantic story.

But it's natural to want to put a little excitement, a little romance, a little love, a few vicarious thrills into our everyday lives and take the parts of an affair that are romantic, that are exciting, that represent our own dreams and make that into the story.

Angelina's and Brad's divorce announcement and Jennifer Aniston's mention at this stage are, unfortunately, just the latest example of how their real life, documented story is a classic illustration of The Affair Playbook, showing the pattern of an affair above and below the surface.

I've been following their story carefully since 2007 because I could see even at that stage in their relationship that they were, along with Jennifer Aniston, a living, documentable example of The Affair Playbook. I had previously outlined the Affair Playbook based on the reported relationships and affairs of other people. It is not difficult to document the Playbook with relevant articles for Angelina, Brad and Jennifer and other 'in the news' politicians, businesspeople, and celebrities since so many details of the lives of famous people are reported in the press.

Does knowing the pattern of an affair help us in any way? Yes it does because almost everyone has been, or is being, affected by an affair in some way. Whether it's how to evaluate what an affair means in the life of someone running for office, or in that person's family. Or how to deal with an affair that's in progress in one's own life or the life of a partner, or a close relative or friend. Or how to understand an affair that's roiling one's workplace.

The catch points in this chronology that are the least discussed are:

- First, the time in an affair when infatuation, intense feelings, disregard of reality and almost an addiction take hold, and
- Second, what children of various ages who are experiencing an affair around them are feeling and thinking.

The Beginning: An Innocent Meeting

Every affair starts with communication between a man and a woman. It is almost always innocent with no special meaning attached to it. However, it is always a positive interaction eliciting a good feeling in one or both. Of course, trillions of non-affairs start this way too.

From the first Brad and Angelina's affair was just like the affair next door—they met at work. The workplace is a natural because by definition it provides a place away from home, and work is a contained, fantasy world all its own. So the setting is fertile ground for an affair. No affair partner begins by thinking, "This month I'm going to have an affair." But each is usually in a state of readiness, a state of dissatisfaction with life as it is.

In Brad and Angelina's case, their jobs also involve personal and physical intimacy, which makes it easier for the relationship to become close. So in their case, hypothetically, it might look something like this:

The day's shooting is done and Angelina turns to Brad.

> Angelina: What do you think about how Doug shot that scene? I'm not happy with it and I'm going to tell him tomorrow. I know everyone just wants to finish and they won't like that I want to do it over.

> Brad: No, no. You're right. I felt the same way. We should reshoot it. You've got all the right instincts, Angie.

Angelina: You think so? Sometimes I doubt myself. But I feel it about that scene.

Brad: I love working with you for just that reason. You know what you feel and you go with it, and you insist on it.

Going Beyond Friendship

"I think a few months in I realized, 'God, I can't wait to get to work,'" Angelina said. "We found joy in working together and a lot of real teamwork. We just became kind of a pair." [as quoted in January 2007 *Vogue*]

A common pre-cursor to an affair is a situation where the man and the woman are working closely and intensely on a workplace project as Brad and Angelina were when they started shooting on *Mr. and Mrs. Smith* in 2004. Without realizing it as it's happening, the woman becomes aware that contact with this man, however brief, has become an important part of her day. She begins paying special attention to her dress and he may too. "I want to look my best today," she may think. "I know I'll see him at the meeting."

This feeling is heightened on a movie set. "It's such an intense thing, being absorbed into the world of a movie." Angelina has said. "It's like discovering you have a fatal illness, with only a short time to live." [*Brangelina: The Untold Story of Brad Pitt and Angelina Jolie*, Ian Halperin p. 61]

"'Because of the film we ended up being brought together to do all these crazy things, and I think we found this strange friendship and partnership that kind of just suddenly happened,'" Angelina said." [Jan. 2007 *Vogue*]

In general, when two people are having an affair, what happens next is that a bond develops between the two that becomes partly sexual. From nothing, to casual compliments meaning nothing, to casual compliments meaning something, to casual intimate comments meaning more, to being together one to one away from the original setting, to feeling intoxicated being together—this is how the affair begins.

At this stage, the interaction between the two expresses only admiring, complimentary, positive, helpful, supportive, ego-boosting and uplifting feelings.

Ever Increasing Closeness

The exchange of thoughts between the two becomes more personal. They share confidences that they're not sharing with anyone else—dreams, hopes, longings, disappointments, family or personal tragedies, what each may feel are unrecognized talents and achievements, unacknowledged sacrifices.

Angelina had a secret dream to own a motel in the middle of nowhere. [*Brangelina*, Ian Halperin p.108]. This is a confidence she might have shared with Brad, and only Brad, as they got to know each other at the beginning of filming of *Mr. and Mrs. Smith*. As Angelina began to feel that Brad understood her, liked her, and wouldn't make fun of way-out ideas—after all, the reaction to a beautiful, rich, world-renowned actress wanting to own a small, no-frills motel miles from anywhere would generally be, 'Why would she want to do that? Maybe she isn't as brilliant and as gorgeous as she seems to be'—Angelina would be unafraid and eager to share this with Brad.

At this stage a man might say to the woman he is drawing closer to, "You know, my wife and I hardly ever have sex."

The Key Act that Moves It Forward, Sometimes Identifiable Only in Retrospect

"Not a lot of people get to see a movie where their parents fell in love." Angelina [*Life & Style* March 15, 2010] "Because you know...six kids. Because I fell in love." Brad Pitt telling *Rolling Stone* magazine [Dec 12, 2008] why *Mr. and Mrs. Smith* was his favorite movie.

One or the other does something deliberate to move the relationship forward. It could involve touching, looking, speaking, or emitting (such as wearing perfume) in a new, closer, more personal way.

In Angelina's case the deliberate act to move it forward could have been something like Angelina giving Brad a passionate kiss when the *Mr. and Mrs. Smith* script simply called for an embrace.

Or it could have been that she or Brad held each other just a little closer than necessary in a scene that involved embracing. On or off the set their eyes could have locked in contact a little longer than necessary.

It is very common for one or both to say that they didn't do anything intentional to start the new relationship. Afterwards they report that it was something beyond oneself, some pre-determined attraction, something spiritual, something destined to be no matter how much they tried not to.

Angelina has said this about the beginning of her other relationships before she knew Brad. Regarding Billy Bob Thornton Angelina said, "And then we came out of that elevator and I just remember, you know, wanting something not to go away. Something went wrong with me in that elevator. Chemical...I became a complete idiot." [*Brangelina*, Ian Halperin, p.165] Halperin also reports what someone observed when Angelina and Billy Bob were having dinner after a day of filming *Pushing Tin*— "There were others seated with them but 'across the table, they talked and a connection was made.'"

At this point it's likely to go forward to an affair unless one or the other or outside circumstances say "Stop".

Meeting Away from the Original Setting

When a man and a woman plan to meet in a place away from where they initially interacted, it means that the relationship has started to take on a life of its own. It is evidence of a need or desire which goes beyond the original reason they had occasion to be together. "Could you help me with my new Ikea furniture?" she says. For Brad and Angelina it might have gone something like this:

It's the end of the day and Brad and Angelina are walking to their dressing room trailers.

> Angelina: I'd love a great glass of wine now. I don't like any of the stuff the studio sent me.

> Brad: Want to go to Louie's? You know he keeps a private area for me for whenever I come in. The guy's great. Never made it on set but he knows how to run a club.

> Angelina: Yes, I'm sick of this place. They didn't bring me any of the stuff I asked for.

> Brad: Louie will get you anything you want. Go change and then we'll go to Louie's.

Action!

Filming for *Mr. and Mrs. Smith* started in LA in January, 2004 and by February, Angelina was meeting Brad at a rented house an insider said. [*Life & Style* March 15, 2010] One particular day, Angie went to visit her mother at L'Ermitage Hotel, where she was living, then was smuggled out of the underground parking lot in a van with blacked-out windows to go meet Brad.

"It was the electrifying love-making that brought Brangelina together," *The New York Post* quoted biographer Halperin as saying. "Brad had never had such incredible sex."

The indication of interest has been expressed— the touch, the word, the sustained eye contact, the perfume—the deliberate act that moved it forward.

This was something just between the two of them. If it happened that other people were around, one of these witnesses may have noticed that a spark flew between the two. But the new couple is oblivious to this.

This is the point when a new couple generally will take action. They know they must keep it secret because one or both of them is married. But the risk in being found out has gone up because they will be meeting away from the original setting, such as the film set or workplace where it was unremarkable for them to be seen together.

However, risk management, restraint and convention have been overpowered by desire, nature and satisfaction.

The Tales the Man Spins

In general at this point in an affair a man will tell his new partner that he and his wife were just good friends and were waiting for the right time to end the marriage--when the kids graduate from high school, when real estate prices go up or when the dog dies.

To drown both his guilt and his partner's, the man continues to propound societally accepted explanations on why their close and secret relationship is NOT breaking up a marriage. The core of the explanation is "My wife is crazy, she doesn't understand me, and the marriage is really over."

He wants to assure the other woman that she is not breaking up a marriage. That's why he tells her the marriage is already over. There is nothing left. Therefore it's not cheating.

Angelina was probably surprised by Jen's reaction to Angelina's admission that she and Brad had fallen in love on the set of *Mr. & Mrs. Smith*. Angelina believed Brad and Jen's marriage was really over, since that's perhaps what Brad told her. But as far as Jen knew at that time, perhaps their marriage was as good as it had ever been. Possibly there were problems between Brad and Jen, as in any marriage, but they worked on solving them.

Like all men at this stage of an affair, Brad was spinning tales to his wife, pretending everything was fine, and to his affair partner to keep her guilt free and assured in their relationship. He wants it all at this stage—the security of marriage, the high of the affair, and the respect of the world.

Present Tense

Angelina said about her relationship with Jonny Lee Miller, "The way we both feel about life is to live in the moment and not live in the future." [*Brangelina*, Halperin p. 66] This is probably how Angelina thought about her relationship with Brad too.

An affair is about the present, marriage is about the future—children growing up, planning to buy a house, looking towards advancement in a job, planning for retirement. Let's say this—you don't talk about annuities in an affair.

Living in the present, especially when it mostly involves having hot sex, there are no problems to deal with. So initially, the affair will always trump the marriage.

Seeds of Destruction

In January, 2010 Brad insisted to Angie that she seek treatment for her emotional demons and physical issues. Brad didn't see all of Angie during the affair period because Angie was savvy enough to conceal the unattractive and extreme parts of her personality. They also were only together for short, intense snippets of time. So, five years after they first met, Brad was dealing with the fallout from what he didn't know was there. He found himself a partner with someone who as *The New York Post* [Sept 22, 2016] described, had "a reputation as a bisexual former heroin junkie and cocaine abuser who once teased that she'd engaged in an incestuous relationship with her own brother."

"The depth of Angelina's forays into lesbianism and drugs are the biggest skeletons she kept in her closet, and the disclosures have left Brad feeling utterly betrayed, said the source." [*National Enquirer*, August 16, 2010]

Now 12 years after they met, some of these same unattractive aspects of Angelina's personality are in the forefront again and are possibly, nay probably, the cause of Angelina's filing for divorce. She kept them secret at the beginning but she couldn't keep them down.

These are all examples of secrecy, the very essence of an affair. Secret then, out in the open now, leading to divorce.

By definition, an affair keeps out reality, which eventually will come through and cause destruction. The emotions, restrictions and enhancements that define an affair contain within them the seeds of destruction.

The seeds of destruction are:

- Secrecy
- Boundless and unrealistic expectations for the future
- The methodology, way of life and habits of an affair
- The creation of a great story built on a foundation of lies
- Generalizing from the courtship to the marriage, and
- The personality of the woman having an affair, who tends to emphasize the positive and feels looking at the negative serves no purpose

For instance, a woman in an affair with a married man might think, "I'd like to ask him if he's told his wife that he's very unhappy in the marriage but then he'll think I don't trust what he's told me about the marriage being over except on paper."

At the beginning of an affair it's very common for both parties to hide these unpleasant truths.

Forced To Choose

At some point one or both of the two women in his life presses the man to make a decision. His wife wants him to break off the affair (if she knows about it), the other woman presses him to get married. He knows he is going to make one of the two women angry and disappointed. He chooses based on whose attractive pull is stronger, who he's more afraid of, and whose anger and devastation he can ignore, deal with and explain away the best.

We know, of course, that Brad chose Angelina. Brad was still in the fantasy period of the affair where everything about Angelina seemed perfect. Brad knew he was going to deal with anger when he told Jennifer he was leaving. Then again when she found out that he was going to live with another woman. Then again when Jennifer realized the other relationship had been going on for some time. And then again when Jennifer was faced with photos showing Brad being a family man with Angelina and her son Maddox.

Brad tried to cut Jennifer's anger off at the pass by being especially nice to her immediately before they split. They went to Anguilla and I saw photos showing them looking lovingly at each other; Brad seems to be really close and caring towards Jennifer and she seems to be sincerely responding.

Jennifer appears to be the sweeter, more accommodating, less secure woman compared to Angelina, who seems to be more demanding, more willing to stand up to criticism and more forceful. Because of each of their characteristics, Brad might have felt he could deal with Jennifer's devastation and hurt more easily. This is a truth about affairs: All kinds of women have affairs but passive women rarely become second wives. [Thomas W. Blume, PhD, Licensed Marriage and Family Therapist in Michigan]

Newspapers began to report that Jennifer didn't want to take time from her career to start a family, the children that Brad always wanted. This created a story line that paints the affair partners in a radiant light and the woman at home as selfish, uncaring and not a good wife.

According to biographer Ian Halperin in *Brangelina* it was Angelina herself who leaked that story. "The first hints of how Angelina planned to do that soon emerged. 'Insiders claim Pitt's desire to start a family and his wife's reluctance to give up her career have caused "intolerable pressures," wrote one newspaper. Many such stories began to appear as the year progressed, all citing "insiders" and all hinting that Aniston was selfishly denying her husband the family he so desperately craved."

The reaction by outsiders: 'No wonder he had to leave.'

How Long Is New New?

On Jan. 7, 2005, Brad and Jen publicly announced their separation. Three months later Brad and Angelina were photographed on a private beach in Kenya.

How long is new new? The answer is two years. If the couple doesn't commit by then, it becomes less and less likely that the man will leave his wife. And two years is also the duration of newness for the new couple.

At the end of two years the marker of holidays, birthdays, vacations and seasons has been experienced more than once and the excitement of life wanes.

In less than two years from when they started filming *Mr. & Mrs. Smith*, while things were still feeling exciting and new, Brad and Angelina became a public couple. Couples generally at this point want to solidify the relationship. The woman wants to keep the man, and the man is proud to have this sexy new woman on his arm.

Once the man has left his wife, he wants to be sure to get married. Men don't want to live alone.

The Outside World Learns That the Man and His Wife Are Separating

"We would like to announce that after seven years together, we have decided to formally separate," read the joint announcement of Brad and Jen's separation. The decision was the result of "much thoughtful consideration" and it was not caused by "any of the speculation reported by the tabloid media" the couple said, adding that they would remain "committed and caring friends with great love and admiration for one another."

"Did you hear that Joe and Sue are getting divorced? They'll always respect and love each other but they just were too different to stay together," everyone says whenever they learn about a couple's split. This is the carefully staged script the man creates to make sure no one thinks he was cheating. But there is always someone else.

It is clear from the Playbook why Brad (and Angelina through Brad) would want the announcement to read this way (This was not because of an affair) but I can only guess, based on the Playbook, why Jennifer would agree to this wording—As famous and as pretty and as rich as she was, she was still worried about seeming 'nice', not angry or vengeful.

"We wrote it [the separation announcement] together and felt very good about it, said Jen in September. We exited this relationship as beautifully as we entered it." [*OK!* May 8, 2006]

It later came out that Brad and Angelina had fallen in love before the separation announcement. They disclosed that they had fallen in love on the set of *Mr. and Mrs. Smith*.

Most couples in an affair want to hide the fact that the new public partnership started with a hidden relationship.

Broadcasting the Story Line

"It's about children. [Anniston] just doesn't want kids right now, and he wants kids." [Ian Halperin, *Brangelina*, p. 231 quoting a story in *The New York Post*]

"A pal said Anniston doesn't want to take the time off to have a kid and she doesn't want to endure the physical effects that giving birth will have on her sexy body," another report said. [Halperin, *Brangelina* p. 231]

"To be intimate with a married man, when my own father cheated on my mother is not something I could forgive," Angelina said. "I could not, could not, look at myself in the morning if I did that." [*Marie Claire* March, 2005]

The man's theme with the other woman even before it is actually an affair is always, "My wife is crazy, she doesn't understand me and the marriage is really over." Angelina may have really believed Brad that the marriage was over in spirit if not legally and therefore she and Brad were NOT cheating.

Angelina could have been aware of Jennifer saying the opposite about having children--"I've never in my life said I didn't want to have children. I did and I do and I will!" [Jennifer Anniston, *Vanity Fair*, Sept. 2005] But maybe Angelina thought that that was what Jennifer was saying now, but not what she was telling Brad earlier.

The man (and in Angelina and Brad's relationship Angelina often takes on the role of the man while Brad is more reticent) makes it clear that this was not an affair. He puts out a story that is so strong and compelling and sympathetic that it eliminates all thoughts of affairs or cheating among those hearing his story.

A key part of the story is that the wife is crazy, selfish and no good. This is the story Angelina put out about Jennifer, that she put her career ahead of making Brad happy, i.e. she wouldn't take time from being in films to do whatever it took to get pregnant and give Brad the family he wanted. The story worked especially well for Angelina because she had been promoting herself as a dedicated mother and a 'mother' to needy children throughout the world so the comparison was dramatic.

Brad went along with this because, as one of his friends said, maybe Brad was thinking of these stories and saying to himself "I need to get out of this marriage, but I want to come out smelling like a rose, so I'm going to let Jen be cast as the ultra-feminist and I'm going to be cast as the poor husband who couldn't get a baby and so had to move on." [*Vanity Fair*, September, 2005]

Many men (who are not in the public eye) avoid the whole question of whether they had sex while they were still married by saying, "It just happened. We just met last week. But we know we're soulmates." Since they don't have the paparazzi tracking their every move, the date is easier to fudge.

"I do. I do." The New Couple Marries or Lives Together

In March of 2005 photos were shot for a 60-page spread in W magazine which featured Angelina and Brad on the cover looking for the entire world like a married couple. They are sitting in a backyard lawn setting playing with several children with beach balls and a wading pool. The look is family but sexy.

Sound the trumpets in the public square—we're a couple. Please recognize us as such. Although Brad and Angelina had not at this point gotten married, we can date their committed relationship from when they were willing to become public, and when Brad committed legally to the adopted children.

In July of 2005, Angie and Brad went together to Ethiopia to adopt Zahara. "Pitt was with Jolie when she arrived to claim the baby and they looked just like a married couple. They were like any couple looking at their child for the first time. Angelina wiped a tear from her eye. They were so happy. They turned to me and said, 'This makes us a whole family,'" said Dr. Tsegaye Berhe, medical director of the Addis Ababa orphanage. This was just six months after Jennifer and Brad announced their split.

Everyone thinks this is the end of the story— There are good feelings in this new union and the outside world is happy to see love triumph over all. The first wife is sitting at home sad and alone but she is out of sight and nobody is thinking about her now. But she's about to get back into the story.

Embellishing the Outside Story Line

"Angie was in the kitchen doing dishes while the kids were running outside. She could watch from the window." [*US Weekly* Nov 23 2009] Of course, this was the window of the $70 million Chateau Miraval estate near Aix-en-Provence, France.

"Brad loves racing around the grounds [of the chateau] with them [Shiloh and Zahara]. Every time the cart hits a bump, Shiloh squeals with delight." [*US Weekly* Nov 23, 2009]

The man confirms again and again to the outside world that this is a marriage that was meant to be and that his first wife, who was never the right person, is doing fine as are his children. Of course, when you're a huge Hollywood star you have a staff of publicists to help you embellish the story line.

Jen played along by trying to show how well she was doing.

Brad and Angelina have seemed desperate to prove they weren't home-wreckers. Just the opposite. They're building a beautiful family together.

"Talk to Angelina long enough, you end up back at the kids." [*Vanity Fair* August, 2010].

This doesn't jive with past quotes from Angie nor with the way she actually lives her life. "Luckily I've found something that replaces a high, and that is my work." [Halperin, *Brangelina*, p.105] "[My father] was only happy when he was doing his work. So I am pretty grounded from that." [Halperin, *Brangelina*, p. 125]

If family were really first, Angelina wouldn't be dragging her children around the world doing a city a day promotional tours for her films. It has also been mentioned many times that nannies and maids do almost all the child care. But to promote an image of totally involved parents the nannies are hidden when photographers are around.

A lot of effort is put into enrolling people in the story line so that all thoughts of cheating are banished. Even six years later Brad was still justifying why he had to leave Jen. *The New York Post* article "MARRIAGE TO JEN THE PITTS: BRAD" [Sept 16, 2011] references Brad's comments to *Parade* Sept 18, 2011 - "I started getting sick of myself sitting on a couch, holding a joint, hiding out....I wasn't leading an interesting life myself. I think my marriage [to actress Jennifer Aniston] had something to do with it."

The new couple is admired for their courage in dropping everything to follow true love, their dedication to each other and their beauty as a radiant couple.

Surprising Signs That
the First Wife is Not Dead Yet

A couple of years into the second marriage, the new wife thinks, "From the day I first met him, all he did was criticize his wife. Now he doesn't like it if I say anything critical about her." If Angelina is like other second wives, she experienced confusion just like this over how Brad felt about Jen.

During the time of the affair, the man has only negative things to say about his wife. But once he has remarried, he doesn't like it if his new wife says anything critical about his first wife. His new wife is confused and baffled by this 180 degree turn. But to this man, his first wife is still part of his history and his children and thus his life. Criticisms of his first wife are then in a way criticisms of him, his children and his judgment in choosing a wife some years ago. During the time of the affair, criticizing his wife makes him look like the noble, suffering husband. It justified and explained everything to himself--"I've suffered for a long time and now I deserve some happiness"--and to his affair partner who thinks--"This is not cheating, his wife is crazy and he deserves better."

The new wife is baffled by the complete contradiction between what he said about his first wife during the affair and what he is saying now. And she is worried because it is the first sign that he wasn't totally truthful when it was just the two of them in their own world and she had no way of verifying the facts about the other parts of his life.

Attraction to Irritation

"The big fights are over their own schedules. Angie is reluctant to take a break from work." [*OK!* Feb 8, 2010]

"Angie has a nomad mentality, but Brad wants to spend more time in [New Orleans] and work on making a change." [*OK!* Feb 8, 2010]

What attracts a man to a woman during an affair can become a source of irritation when they are married.

In an affair, there is a limited amount of time they can spend together and it is all spent focused on the other one.

But things have changed as it's gone from the affair to the marriage.

For instance, if an affair couple meets at work, the man may find the woman's hard work attractive. Later, when they are married, he might come to resent the time she spends at work and away from him.

Why? Two factors that fueled the fantastical feelings of the affair are each going in the wrong direction. Newness has decreased and time together has increased. Newness is a large factor in attraction. Now that newness is starting to get old, attraction lessens, even if the woman is Angelina and the man is Brad.

The increased amount of time together now that they are married means that an irritating factor which in the affair period might have been overlooked, or overcome by passion, is now magnified because they are together more.

Irritation to Attraction

"[Brad's] long kept an active eye on what Jen is doing and whom she's dating." " 'He is always calling their mutual friends and asking after her,' says a pal. 'Brad knows about pretty much everything Jen does.'"[*OK!* Feb 8, 2010]

Not only is the first wife not dead yet, she may even turn from a source of irritation to a source of attraction. Now the ex-wife is the mysterious, attractive one who may consume all the man's thoughts, exactly the way he felt about the mistress, especially in the first year. She is the one with an air of mystery about her because her ex-husband doesn't know what is going on in her life. His new wife has become ordinary and 'every day' by comparison because he does see her every day.

"I love him, I love him not." says Jen
"I love her, I love her not." says Brad
"He loves her, he loves her not."
says Angie

The Playbook predicts that this may have happened, a yo-yoing between feelings of hurt, anger, disgust, distance and loss of desire for the other one and feelings of love, affection, comfort, friendship, and a desire to be 'in touch'.

Even six years after their separation and divorce, Jen and Brad might have been going back and forth with their feelings towards each other.

But because the Playbook also insists on a black and white outside story line, and dictates what roles everyone is to take, we may not hear about these contradictory feelings of human emotion.

So probably neither Brad nor Jen expected this. Not Brad as the secret, exciting relationship with Angelina began and became binding, nor Jen when Brad told her he was leaving, nor when she found out that he fell in love with Angelina long before he spoke divorce to her. Nor did Angelina expect to have to deal with Brad's feelings towards Jen after Brad and Jen were divorced.

If Brad is like most men in the Affair Playbook, he is going back and forth. On the one hand, he would want to go back to Jennifer because he is comfortable with her, because he has shared so much of life with her, and because she has a steady, girl-next-door personality. On the other hand, he would want to stay with Angelina since he gave up a lot when he made the decision to leave Jennifer and he would want to continue the high of sex with Angelina, the new adventures she has brought to his life and the joy of children and a family. He would look foolish at that point to say, in effect, that after all the trauma and the loss it was a big mistake. And he appears to genuinely love his children and wouldn't want to give up being a constantly present father.

Every man is torn by the forces pulling in two directions that can never openly co-exist or be reconciled.

And it continued into 2016 after Angelina filed for divorce. Brad got in touch with Jennifer, a source of familiarity, comfort and support in his time of shock, sadness and fear of the future, especially regarding his desire to be a close father to his children. [*OK!* Oct. 17, 2016]

The Seeds of Destruction Begin to Sprout

The very things which define an affair are also the seeds of destruction which most commonly sprout when the affair ends and becomes a marriage.

Angie and Brad were showing each other their best side in the limited time they had together in the affair, and so didn't know each other as well as they thought.

"Who are you? I don't know you anymore! Our life together has been nothing but lies!" Brad lashed out at Angelina according to sources talking to The Enquirer. These sources told *The Enquirer* that Brad got an early tip-off about what's in Andrew Morton's book, *Angelina*, and it left him sickened. [*National Enquirer* August 16, 2010]

Sometimes during the affair the man or the woman will do things that they're really not comfortable with or could not sustain long-term just to please the other one or to keep the other one as an affair partner. For instance, a woman may perform certain sexual acts during the affair to make her partner happy. But after they're married, she reverts to her comfort level, leaving her new husband baffled and displeased.

Now that Angelina has 'caught' Brad, she doesn't hesitate to express her true feelings. For instance, she doesn't like living in New Orleans. Likewise during the affair period and in the two years thereafter, Brad did things to please Angelina and to keep her which really didn't reflect his genuine interests and desires. He traveled the world with Angie and went from one home to the other, dragging the children with them. "Now according to an American insider Brad is tired of traveling and ready to slice up his frequent flier card and settle in New Orleans." [*US Weekly* Feb 1 2010]

It's inevitable that there are going to be changed feelings like this as the passionate, fantastical feelings of the affair lessen and the ups and downs of everyday life intrude on the relationship.

In 2013 Angie and Brad had a major crisis of everyday life to deal with. As Angelina described in her op-ed in *The New York Times* (May 14, 2013), she came to grips with her mother, grandmother and great-grandmother's deaths from ovarian cancer at relatively young ages and how this put her at greater risk for the same fate, along with her having a certain gene that put her at even greater risk. Being the mother of six young children made her feel the fear and worry that much more intensely. Because of this gene she is at greater risk for both ovarian cancer and breast cancer and Angelina decided on a double mastectomy which is thought to reduce a woman's risk of breast cancer substantially. She also decided on reconstructive surgery to be done not long after the mastectomy. Then she decided to have her ovaries removed which would reduce her risk of ovarian cancer significantly.

There are no reports of Angie and Brad discussing these risks and fears during the affair. Angie may not have even been aware of what her risks were or what steps she could take to reduce them. Most of all in an affair everything is focused on the positive.

Also these surgeries affected Angie's and, undoubtedly Brad's, feelings and realities of femininity and sex and more children. In general, (and this is an opinion) men don't deal well with sickness. At the beginning of this crisis Brad's genuine love and concern for Angie were, undoubtedly, dominant. Then his concern for her as the mother of his children. Then his concern for himself and the fear of losing his partner. Then there is societal pressure on him, especially as a famous actor and man of the world, to express nothing but loving concern for Angie, and nothing but thoughts like, "She is the same woman to me, no matter what surgeries she has had and what exactly her body looks like." But he may not really feel that way.

Then the constant worry, extra responsibilities and changes in his life take their toll. He may have felt Angie was less sexy after the surgeries. And he may have felt left out because all the attention was on Angie.

It's not hard to see the tensions and conflicts this could engender which never would have even been mentioned during the affair period.

Soulmates?

Like all women in her situation Angelina, both during the affair and after, likely had doubts about whether they were really soulmates. In spite of the totally positive story the man always presents to his mistress, she still asks herself, "Is this really love or just an infatuation?", "Is he just using me for sex?", "What am I doing to his wife?", "Is this really different than an affair?", "Will he do it again?".

The New York Post reported in September 2016 that "Jolie was very jealous of Pitt being around other women, including his *Allied* co-star Marion Cotillard. Jolie's paranoia is understandable, as it's alleged that she had an affair with Pitt during the filming of *Mr. & Mrs. Smith* in 2004, when he was married to Jennifer Aniston."

"Deep down [Jen] wonders if someday they might get back together. So does Angelina. 'It still gnaws at her that Brad could decide he made a huge mistake, leaving Jen for her,' says a family friend." [*Star* June 21, 2010]

Just as every second wife asks herself, Angelina was racked with doubts—"Will he do it again with someone else? Will he go back to his first wife?"

Expressing this fear and uncertainty about what may happen in a phrase I haven't heard before is Wendy Williams in *Life & Style*, "Sometimes how you get him is how you lose him." [*Life & Style*, Oct 10, 2016]

One Big Happy Family or
One Big Family To Care For

"The reality of having a big family is so different than their dream," says a pal…Things are tense between Brad and Angelina, and the kids are fighting more than ever." [*In Touch* August 17, 2009]

In the affair period each one fills in the blanks with positive attributes. It's natural. The high feelings of sex and love make it easy to assume that everything else will also be as magical.

During their affair when Angelina had no idea what kind of father Brad would be and Brad could not be present with Angelina and Maddox in a true parenting environment, each one imagined the other as the perfect parent. But each had a different vision of what the perfect parent was like.

Different parenting styles are one surprise because neither one could meet the other's children, or see what kind of a parent the other one was until the relationship came out into the open which may have been just a short time before the new marriage.

In late 2016, after the divorce announcement, Angelina's and Brad's different parenting styles were mentioned as one of main causes of the divorce. "Still, the two struggled about their diverging parenting styles. 'They started fighting because Brad thought Angie was too laid back,' the source says. 'She doesn't care if the kids do chores. She just wants them to be free to do whatever they want.'...'Brad wanted more consequences for bad behavior. With Angie's approach the kids never learned. That's when Brad would get frustrated and yell.'...'Jolie "definitely never yells" at the children , says the source. "She would plead or not make the kids follow through." ' [*People*, Oct 17, 2016]

"Though Pitt was the stricter of the two, several sources say he never got physical with the kids....He would say 'Hey this isn't how you should be right now, what's wrong?' He doesn't bully or get mean.' " [*People*, Oct 17, 2016]

The Show Must Go On: Burnishing the Embellishment of the Outside Story Line

The romance of true love has hit the reality of true love — there are always some problems. In originally propounding the outside story line, the man went on the offensive to head off any negative impressions by outsiders before they could take hold. Now, some hints of trouble in the new marriage have gotten out. He has to play defense — burnish the embellishments he created before — and offense — put out some new embellishments.

In Brad and Angelina's case, since Angelina often takes on the role of the man this involves heavy work by her too. Plus their creative and financial success depends on their fans having a wonderful, romantic story to hold onto.

"We have each other's back." [*People*, August 2, 2010]

Angelina was very successful in putting out the beautiful story that her relationship with Brad allowed her to have success on all fronts including being a loving parent and a sexy wife to Brad.

For eleven years, Angelina and Brad have been in the headlines as a perfect couple, even as there were also many hints of trouble. Most people go along with the happy storyline, preferring to enjoy vicarious thrills.

Brad, like all men in this situation, was trapped. He couldn't get out of this marriage without looking foolish. While, if he stayed, he could never be himself again.

He had at least four contradictory story lines he had to keep going:

- The story he told to his new wife pre-affair and as the affair progressed
- The story he told to his ex-wife to justify his leaving to himself and to her
- The story he told to the outside world and
- The real world story which created itself and which he could not control.

He has spun such a web of lies there is no one with whom he can really let down. This is one reason he sometimes does it again, because a new woman is someone he can let down with, just as it was with his present wife when she was new.

This is where the man finally realizes the true consequences of the Playbook.

But Brad never expected that Angelina would take action.

The Past and the Future Collide

At this point, the pressure inside the marriage is great. It can't continue this way. And yet the man (and possibly the woman) feels trapped. Some kind of explosion is likely.

In the case of Brad and Angelina, it was Angelina who took the decisive step.

When Angelina filed for divorce, Brad may have felt like he had his power as a man taken away. Leaving the marriage should have been his decision.

Most of all because of the circumstances that Angelina said led to the filing, he can't see his children whenever he wants and in a normal family setting. This also is an attack on his manhood, on his power and on his self-image, and his public image of being a good father.

It could be that Angelina has 'someone else', or maybe two someone elses. Men, and women too, rarely leave to live alone.

What Will Happen Next?

Will Brad marry again? Yes he will because he'll have plenty of opportunity and he won't want to be alone.

Will Angelina marry again? Probably yes, at some point in the future because she will want to know that she has attracted a man who loves her so much that he is willing to make a permanent commitment to her.

What is the future for the kids?

Angie and Brad and many other parents going through divorce proceedings say they want to do whatever is best for the children regardless of anything else. But they've already done what's almost guaranteed not to be best for the children--establishing a relationship built on secrecy, lies and abandoned commitments.

The Jolie-Pitt children were at first living with only infrequent time with their father because Brad was under investigation for possibly abusing Maddox on a plane flight. This must have caused the children great feelings of insecurity, loss and confusion.

The children have new nannies because Angelina, out of fear of staff leaking information to Brad, has "fired all of the kids' nannies." [*Star*, Oct 17, 2016] Relatives, friends, nannies or other household employees a child knows and likes give a feeling of security and having someone they can turn to. We can understand Angelina's fears of leaks which could affect the court's permanent custody decisions but it is not good for the children to all of a sudden have to adjust to new people.

Vanity Fair reported in December, 2016, that "Pitt's legal team alleges [in court documents] that Jolie is 'continu[ing] to place her own interests above those of the minor children and to disregard their privacy rights when she believes it may benefit her.'"

The children's education is probably disrupted. They are taught by tutors but if the tutors have changed then that is not good for the children. The part of their education that involves traveling and learning about other cultures was disrupted because Angelina and Brad had to stay within range of Los Angeles child protection services.

In many families financial problems would become a serious issue because the parents' work hours and location would be affected. Brad and Angelina's work and careers probably are being affected but money is not an issue for them.

The situation that the children and Angelina and Brad are in has some additional negative effects for the children. Some will be with them for a long time.

As a society we are not acknowledging this. Acknowledgment would help as a start to see how affairs have far-reaching and long term effects.

www.ingramcontent.com/pod-product-compliance
Lightning Source LLC
Chambersburg PA
CBHW060659280326
41933CB00012B/2250